DANGEROUSLY COOL PLACE...

coke OR pepsi?

GIRL!

C or P

whaddya have
to say?

random thoughts
cool Q&A's
very ~~scientific~~
quizzes

coke **OR** pepsi?

GIRL!

Written and designed by
Mickey & Cheryl Gill

FINE print
P U B L I S H I N G

Fine Print Publishing Company
P.O. Box 916401
Longwood, Florida 32971-6401

ISBN: 978-189295147-2

This book is printed on acid-free paper.
Created in the U.S.A. & Printed in China

2 3 5 7 9 10 8 6 4 1

coke-or-pepsi.com

If you find this book write A cool Message here

and send it back to me. Thx,

owner's name here

1. Find out some pretty HILARIOUS stuff about your friends

2. Take a quiz that's anything but ordinary

3. Make a super cool accessory out of a page in the book

4. Give a shout-out to a friend

5. Save the world

And finally rip some pages out, write some random stuff, and hang it somewhere, anywhere. Oops, that's 6 reasons.

So get busy —
life as you know it
is about to change.

coke-or-pepsi.com

your initials

Most people don't know that I

4 those Xtra long names

I have a super scary
- [ ] scream
- [ ] laugh
- [ ] burp
- [ ] other

Last person u lol with?

Trace your thumb or BIG TOE here. Finish drawing it.

I'm way better at

than most people.

Empty your backpack or bag. Look for something small. Tape it here.

om things about me & the world around me.

Here's your chance graffiti girl.

Paint, lipstick, or nail polish

what you've been dying to shout out loud!

WHADDYA THINK
OF WHEN
U SEE
THE WORD...

(IT CAN BE ANOTHER WORD, A SENTENCE,
A MEMORY,
OR EVEN AN ENTIRE STORY.)

HEART

BARK

GREEN

BUTTERFLY

CROWN

CROWN

BUTTERFLY

GREEN

BARK

HEART

RITE DOWN THE ANS

OK,
WHAT DOES YOUR
BEST FRIEND
THINK OF WHEN
SHE HEARS
THE SAME WORDS?

The very scientific test for LOVE

Color a petal red each time your crush makes eye contact, smiles at, or says something nice about you (or says something wonderful about you to someone else).

Color a petal black for each time he has a chance but doesn't make eye contact, smile, or talk to you. Ugh!

Love Study Results from ~~Noted~~ Experts

lots of red petals

He definitely loves you and you'll probably get married, have five kids, and live in a big house someday.

half red petals, half black petals

Hmmm. He probably doesn't LOVE you, but let's not rule out LIKE just yet.

lots of black petals

It's most likely 1 of these 3.

a. He's just not that into you. His loss!

b. You're way cooler than he is, and he knows it.

c. He's noticed that you're always staring at him and scribbling in this book. And it's really freakin' him out!

IF YOUR FRIEND IS HAVING A SUPER BAD DAY

this book could really help.

Cut out the mask to the right. Cut out eye holes.
Thread strings thru holes and tie it around your face.
(Wearing all black with tights too would be a nice touch.)
Go see your friend. Tell her

I'm **Super Pits!**
A.K.A. - Miss Cherry Maraschino,
and I've come to save the day!

Yeah, it's stupid. Bet your friend will laugh though.

The Girl in the
ron-ic Mask

Cut out & wear for those last-minute costume parties or just cuz.

Another pair of eyes

Can't take my eyes off of you

Keep your eye on the ball

More than meets the eye

Look into my eyes

4 ur eyes only

IN THE BLINK OF AN EYE

In the minds eye

in the twinkling of an eye

COULDN'T BELIEVE MY EYES

Only have eyes for U

MY LIFE IS SCRAP

Look for scraps of stuff from your daily life
(gum wrappers, fruit labels, notes, and on & on).
Tape them to this page. Write down where they came from.

i'm watching you

If you're right-handed, draw your best friend with your left hand. If you're a lefty, draw your bf with your right.

Draw a picture of yourself without using your hands. Hold a black marker between your teeth or toes.

She's soooo boring.
Dress her in your favorite outfit.

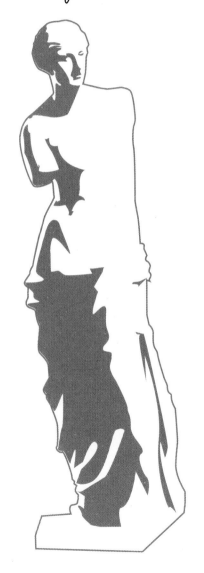

READ MY LIPS

1. Apply lipstick or lipgloss to lips.
2. Blot below.
3. Write name of kissable color next to it.
4. Repeat with other colors.

Now you have a lipstick log

Leave this page blank

IF YOU'RE FEELING SUPER SAD THIS BOOK COULD REALLY HELP YOU.

Tear out this page

Crumble it up over and over again

Roll it between your hands until it's really soft

Wipe away your tears

Write the first letter of your first name here ✭

Fill in the blanks with words or phrases that begin with this letter.

1. something you like to do _____

2. one of your favorite foods _____

3. excuse 4 not doing homework _____

4. animal _____

5. something in ur room _____

6. item of clothing _____

7. word u say a lot _____

8. person's last name _____

9. something sweet _____

10. something salty _____

ok, write your last name here

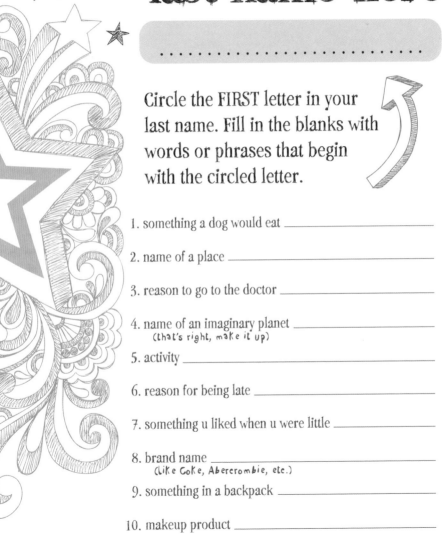

Circle the FIRST letter in your last name. Fill in the blanks with words or phrases that begin with the circled letter.

1. something a dog would eat _____

2. name of a place _____

3. reason to go to the doctor _____

4. name of an imaginary planet _____
   (that's right, make it up)

5. activity _____

6. reason for being late _____

7. something u liked when u were little _____

8. brand name _____
   (Like Coke, Abercrombie, etc.)

9. something in a backpack _____

10. makeup product _____

DO NOT WRITE ON THIS PAGE. YOU'LL SEE WHY LATER.

WRITE SOMETHING HERE IN THE SECRET VAULT.
SOON, YOU'LL LOCK IT UP.

wish one

wish two

Make a wish on a shooting star. Write it on the tail. Poke holes in all the little circles.

Then glue or tape this page to the page behind it.

wish
three

wish four

wish
five

Glue or
tape this page
to the page
behind it.

DRAW SOME-
THING BEHIND
THE SECRET
DOOR. YOU'LL
BE CLOSING
IT SOON.

THIS PAGE!

WHY YOU DON'T WANT TO WRITE ON

←TURN THAT PAGE OVER TO SEE

COKE or PEPSI?

Ask yourself. Ask your friends.

draw it

1. What's your 1st memory? _____

2. ◯ Nutritious fruit smoothie ◯ Decadent chocolate milkshake

3. CONFESSION TIME

Something u said u like because everyone else did (but secretly

you didn't)? _____ ◯ Huh?

4. What cool class do u wish your school offered? _____

5. I would never give up
   ◯ my cell phone
   ◯ the Internet
   ◯ toilet paper!

6. Something you do that bugs other
   people but you still do it? _____

   _____

7. Finish this sentence. I Love _____ .

8. ◯ Kill ◯ Run from ◯ Trap & release roaches. Ick!

9. What other language would u like 2 speak? _____

10. Had onion breath? ◯ Yes ◯ No How 'bout garlic? ◯ Yes ◯ No

COKE OR PEPSI?

Ask yourself. Ask your friends.

1. If you were a crayon, what color would you be? _____

2. Like to have your hair brushed? ○ Yes, feels great! ○ No way

3. Person you've talked to the most today? _____

4. Sitting on a seat that's been warmed by someone else?
○ Creepy ○ Fine, no prob

5. Favorite room color and Y? _____

6. Yummier smell?
○ Movie theater popcorn ○ Chocolate in a candy store

7. How do you feel about raisins? ○ Love 'em ○ Hate 'em **y?**

8. Pets sleep in bed with you?
○ Yep, I snuggle with them ○ No ○ No pets

9. I ALWAYS forget _____.

10. What's on your bedroom floor? _____

_____

Write down as
many of the
lyrics as you
can remember.

_____
. . . .
. . . .
. . . .
. . . .

COKE OR PEPSI?

Ask yourself. Ask your friends.

1. Last celebrity you read about? _____

2. Mixed vegetables ○ should be banned ○ are tasty!

3. Something you've tried & will never try/do again?

   _____

4. Ever run a lemonade stand? ○ Nope ○ Yep

5. I'm in love with _____.

6. What's in your perfect taco? _____

7. Who makes u laff the hardest? _____

8. What weird food combo do you love? _____

   _____

9. Ever been on crutches? ○ No ○ Yes. What 4? _____

   _____

10. What's your absolute most favorite song right now?

Start your own
Paper Chain
letter

Emily — My cat — Brittany — Soccer — Chocolate

1. Write your name & something you love on a link.

2. Ask friends to do the same.

3. Cut out the links and tape together, like a chain.

4. Hang the paper chain and sign. (Turn 2 pages to find sign.)

5. Ask more friends to add links.

Check out paper chain letter at coke-or-pepsi.com

This is a
Paper Chain letter ☺

Name _____

loves _____
person, place, thing, activity

Name _____

loves _____
person, place, thing, activity

Name _____

loves _____
person, place, thing, activity

Name _____

loves _____
person, place, thing, activity

Name _____

loves _____
person, place, thing, activity

Name _____

loves _____
person, place, thing, activity

don't break the chain.

Name _____ loves _____ person, place, thing, activity

Name _____ loves _____ person, place, thing, activity

Name _____ loves _____ person, place, thing, activity

Name _____ loves _____ person, place, thing, activity

Name _____ loves _____ person, place, thing, activity

Name _____ loves _____ person, place, thing, activity

Name _____ loves _____ person, place, thing, activity

Hang this sign next to your paper chain

THIS IS A PAPER CHAIN

LETTER. WRITE YOUR NAME

& SOMETHING YOU ♥ ON A
or someone

LITTLE PIECE OF PAPER

& ADD IT TO THE CHAIN.
Don't break the chain.

WRITE A RAP
ABOUT SOMETHING DRAMATIC (OR NOT) THAT HAPPENED TODAY.

I'm
Just
SA

Let your friends say whatever they want in chalk.

YIN'

Erase. Start all over again.

WHICH IS THE WORST?

Rank them from 1-10.

10 being the most humiliating EVER!

Ask around. Did any of these ever happen to anyone you know?

☐ Made your big solo debut in front of entire school and forgot the lyrics to your song.

☐ Got a little too excited at a school pep rally and split your pants. Rip!

☐ Walked into the boys bathroom by mistake (and it's NOT empty). *Wrong door!*

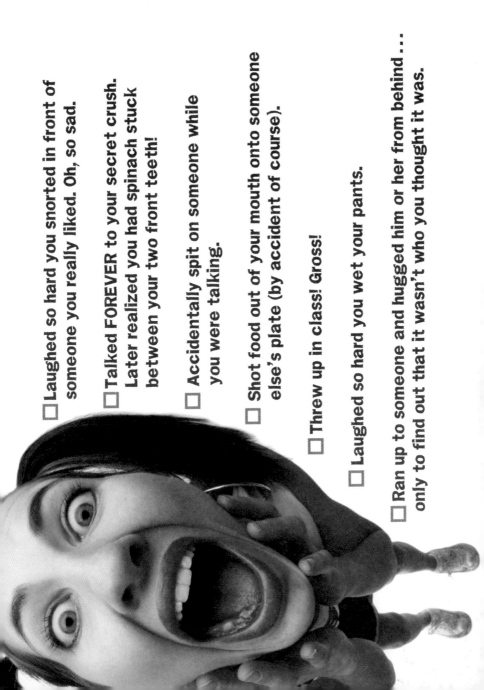

☐ Laughed so hard you snorted in front of someone you really liked. Oh, so sad.

☐ Talked FOREVER to your secret crush. Later realized you had spinach stuck between your two front teeth!

☐ Accidentally spit on someone while you were talking.

☐ Shot food out of your mouth onto someone else's plate (by accident of course).

☐ Threw up in class! Gross!

☐ Laughed so hard you wet your pants.

☐ Ran up to someone and hugged him or her from behind . . . only to find out that it wasn't who you thought it was.

Put this book under your

Write down a dream
the next morning.
(Keep this book
under your pillow
until you remember
a dream.)

Wear this Book

Make a cut paper cuff bracelet

1. Cut out a silver or gold cuff.

2. Cut out wings or jewels.

3. Wrap cuff around wrist, tape together, and cut off any extra cuff.

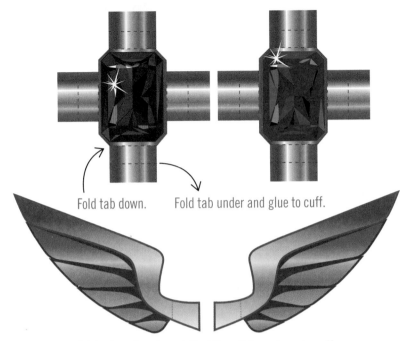

Fold tab down.   Fold tab under and glue to cuff.

Fold tab under along dotted lines & tape down to cuff.

The itsy-bitsy Luv ya note.

1. Write a note in the above.

2. Cut it out.

3. Fold each side in like this.

4. Then fold top down.

5. Fold the flap up and seal with a sticker.

Write something you want to forget about.

Have you ever stuck a piece of gum under a desk?

If yes, that's gross.

Well, here's your chance to do it if you never have or if you need to get it out of your system 1 last time.

1. Chew some gum.

2. Stick it here ⟶ under desk.

3. Cut left page in half, following the dotted line.

4. Fold over and stick to gum.

WHO WOU TO

Choose wisely (that super smart brainiac from school might be better than the cute kid at the smoothie place)

☞ ... were caught in the path of an oncoming twister ?

☞ ... needed a partner for a popular TV dance show ?

... had 1 day to convince aliens not take over the world ?

,D YOU CHOOSE
E WITH YOU IF
YOU...

Ask yourself.

Ask your friends.

my best friend

my brother

my fave movie star

☞ **Why?** _____

hottie down the street

_____

_____

☞ **Why?** _____

_____

_____

☞ **Why?** _____

_____

_____

For your pouty pucker, do you prefer...

- ○ #1 chapstick
- ○ 2b or not 2b. luscious lipstick
- ○ c. pink lipgloss
- ○ Triple D. all of the above

What feels most like you?

- ○ #1 t-shirt and jeans
- ○ 2b or not 2b. mismatched pieces I put together
- ○ c. trendy skirt & top
- ○ Triple D. all of the above

To satisfy the hungry girl within what sounds best?

- ○ #1 burger & fries
- ○ 2b or not 2b. Moo Shu pork
- ○ c. chicken & veggies
- ○ Triple D. all of the above

A cool Saturday would be

- ○ #1 movie with a few friends
- ○ 2b or not 2b. hang out with best friend
- ○ c. mall with a group of friends
- ○ Triple D. all of the above

Worst nightmare?

- ○ #1 friendship drama
- ○ 2b or not 2b. being told I'm average
- ○ c. nothing to wear
- ○ Triple D. all of the above

CHECK OUT
WWW.COKE-OR-PEPSI.COM
FOR EXTREMELY UNSCIENTIFIC,
NEVER TESTED BEFORE RESULTS.

coke OR pepsi?

Paint each toenail with different nail polish colors you like.

Check out your shoes. Write

_____ _____

_____ _____

_____ _____

Write the
color name
on each toe.

ll the different brand names here.

If you need a good little laugh
(you know, not the tear-inducing, wet your
pants, I can't breathe laughter), try this

{ Close your eyes and move a
finger up and down this list
and stop. Open your eyes and
write the word you landed
on in the space below. }

{ Now, do the same
thing with this list
of words. }

A

juicy
green
slippery
captain
sticky
lady

B

hairball
spittle bug
dumplings
gym socks
dung beetle
turkey legs

_____
Word from list A

_____
Word from list B

Write this word combo
on different surfaces
this week. Just cuz.

annals of the "Not-so-Secret" Secret Society

What's the
Scariest
thing that's ever happened
to you?

Ask your friends. Ask yourself. Write the stories down.

I heard footsteps behind me.

I walked into class and didn't know there was a test.

turn

I borrowed my sister's shirt without asking her and she...

I swear I saw a shadow following me...

Now, ask each friend to give
you an awesome
"I'M SCARED TO DEATH"
scream.
(Don't do it in public.)
Vote on the Best.

The
N-S-s
Secret Society
Awards

Name

the title of the best
delivery of a
blood-curdling,
horror movie-
worthy
Scream!

What's the most
Embarrassing
thing that's ever happened
to you?

Ask your friends. Ask yourself. Write the stories down.

I couldn't remember the name of...

_____

_____

_____

_____

_____

_____

_____

I slipped on some ice cream at

turn

the mall and landed on my butt!

I went to school with a price tag hanging from my shirt.

If I spit on the guy who sits next to me...

Is this a word?

Who has the Embarrassing-est story ever?

N-S-S

Secret Society

Name

is officially Miss Mortified!

Do You Risk the Embarrassment?

What would u or your friends be willing to do on a dare?

wear a shirt inside out for a whole day?

fill in space between eye-brows with a brow pencil, creating a unibrow?

tape toilet tissue to the bottom of your shoe and drag it around the mall?

wear a homemade "women's restroom" sign on your back to a football game?

call someone by the wrong name repeatedly?

What's the
Worst Pain
you've ever felt?

Ask your friends. Ask yourself. Write the stories down.

allergic and it crushed me.   I tripped

I was

because I

to a friend

give my kitty away

I had to

and busted my head open on a doorknob.

turn ➤➤ O

I accidentally squirted lemon into a gash...

Who has the most excruciatingly Painful story?

N-S-S

Secret Society

Name

is the Queen of Pain!

How many of these have you (or friends) felt the Pain of?

- ○ bee sting
- ○ wasp sting
- ○ jellyfish sting
- ○ ant bite
- ○ mosquito bite
- ○ spider bite
- ○ shark bite
- ○ dog bite
- ○ cat bite
- ○ vampire bite
- ○ snake bite
- ○ little kid bite
- ○ cat scratch
- ○ sunburn
- ○ busted lip
- ○ broken arm
- ○ broken nose

- ○ broken leg
- ○ broken finger
- ○ broken toe
- ○ broken heart
- ○ bump on the head
- ○ iron burn
- ○ stove burn
- ○ paper cut
- ○ gaping wound
- ○ stitches
- ○ spanking! Yow!
- ○ splinter
- ○ pink eye!
- ○ earache
- ○ toothache
- ○ sore throat
- ○ needle shot

You have a pair of Rollerblades, a bowl of spaghetti & meatballs and a rake.

What could you and a friend do with this stuff?
Ask around. Write your answers down.

_____

_____

_____

_____

_____

_____

you
must
think
outside
the
b
o
x

Have trouble writing papers for school?

1. Cut this lightbulb out. 2. Thread a string thru hole and hang from ceiling. 3. Grab a friend and sit under it. You'll have an idea in no time or at least a cool decoration.

AS of

Today's date

what was the last LOL the thing u about?

What the thing was last U ate?

Do you really want to know?

What was the last thing you stepped in? (think hard)
or on

What was the last thing you cried about?

What's the most awesome pet (or wild animal) story, trick, whatever that you've heard.

Write the stories here.

_____

_____

_____

_____

_____

_____

_____

Ask friends what's the funniest pet name they've ever heard. List them here.

Circle the most laff out loud one!

the
_____
name   kind of animal or breed

the
_____
name   kind of animal or breed

the
_____
name   kind of animal or breed

the
_____
name   kind of animal or breed

the
_____
name   kind of animal or breed

the
_____
name   kind of animal or breed

the
_____
name   kind of animal or breed

the
_____
name   kind of animal or breed

the
_____
name   kind of animal or breed

the
_____
name   kind of animal or breed

THIS IS A QUIZ.

IT'S OPEN BOOK. ASK YOUR FRIENDS FOR HELP. THERE'S NO TIME LIMIT.

1. Write down everything you like to EAT.

2. Write down anything you HATE to do.

3. Write down everything you LOVE. (people, pets, sports, etc.)

Circle your **ABSOLUTE FAVE!** Write it here.

Circle the **WORST!** Write it here.

Circle 1 of your **LOVES.** Write it here.

You're a(n) _____ eating, _____ hating, _____ loving person.

SPRAY WHAT'S

Use paint, lipstick,
nail polish, whatever...
write what you've been dying to say.

Stuck in a boring situation?

Give LIFE to these Inkblots

Add eyes, nose, ears, hats, boots, you name it.
Give them a car, scooter, or plane so they can escape this page.

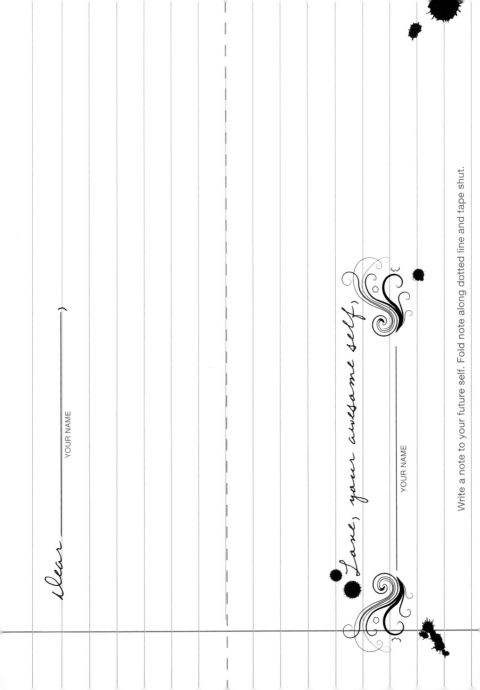

Dear _____

YOUR NAME

Love, your awesome self,

_____

YOUR NAME

Write a note to your future self. Fold note along dotted line and tape shut.

Note to future self

DRAW YOUR BEST DOODLES
IN THIS SPACE.

WRITE DOWN HILARIOUS ☺ STORIES, LATEST CRUSH NEWS, WHATEVER U WANT. 👉

TAPE PICS, TICKETS, & NOTES DOWN TOO. ➡

STICK THIS --->

STUFF UP

IN YOUR

LOCKER,

BEDROOM,

OR

WHEREVER

Go to
coke-or-pepsi.com
to download more copies.

Cut out and tape to your locker, bedroom door or wherever, just to annoy people.

Cut out and tape to your bedroom door.

Cut out and tape to your bedroom door.

Sun-Fri

24 HOURS
6 DAYS A WEEK

Sat

ALL HOURS
EXCEPT 3-3:15 AM

RESTROOM

Sat

3 AM - 3:15 AM

Cut out and tape to your bathroom door.

VISITORS

PLEASE
REGISTER AT
SECURITY OFFICE

Cut out and tape to your bedroom door.

ONE
WAY

→ **MINE**

Cut out and tape wherever you want. You are the boss.

NO
CUTE SHIRT,
CUTE SHOES,
N⊝
ENTRY

Cut out and tape to your bedroom door. Keep out.

Please Take a Number

1 2 3 4 5 6 7

Cut out sign. Cut along dotted lines. Tape anywhere you want.

Tear out this page.

Cut out pocket and
tape or glue to inside
back cover of book.

This is where I stopped.

Tear out this page.

Cut
bookmark
out
and
fold
along
dotted
line.

GIRL! Creators

Mickey
Something unusual about u?
Grew up on a catfish farm.
Coke or Pepsi? Coke, always.
Collect anything? Converses.

Cheryl
Something you like that most
people don't? TV ads.
Collect anything? Scarves and
little soap figurines. Weird.
Whaddya love? Asking people
lots of questions.

Hawkeye (our muse)
Fave thing to do?
Sneak out of the house.
Coke or Pepsi? Huh?
What scares you? Plastic bags.